CAREER
MAPPING

the publishing CIRCLE

admin@ThePublishingCircle.com
or
THE PUBLISHING CIRCLE
Regarding: Dorothy Tannahill-Moran
19215 SE 34th Street
Suite 106-347
Camas, Washington 98607

CAREER MAPPING: PLANNING YOUR CAREER ON PURPOSE /
DOROTHY TANNAHILL-MORAN
SECOND EDITION

ISBN 978-1-947398-09-2

Book design by Michele Uplinger

PRAISE FOR CAREER MAPPING

"Written for people who see themselves as introverts or socially reluctant, this book makes an intelligent contribution to the discussion of networking, an activity of dramatically increasing importance for personal stability in an increasingly uncertain professional world."

Martin Yate, CPC
NEW YORK TIMES BEST-SELLING AUTHOR,
"KNOCK EM DEAD— SECRETS & STRATEGIES FOR SUCCESS
IN AN UNCERTAIN WORLD"

"Leaving your career to chance is risky and hoping your employer will provide you with opportunities to grow is unadvised in today's work climate. Proactive career development, through vision, goal setting, and most importantly, accountability resources will ensure you embark on the path towards your dreams and find some happiness along the way. This easy-to-digest book makes it do-able. CAREER MAPPING won't leave you feeling overwhelmed as you go through the clearly defined steps. It contains bite-sized nuggets illustrated by stories to help hit the key points home."

Hannah Morgan
CAREER SHERPA

"Dorothy delivers smart, actionable advice that gets results in her new career management book. Career Mapping is imperative—now more than ever—for anyone looking to accelerate professionally and maintain more control in this rapidly changing economy. The book is a "must read" and Dorothy is a "must follow." I highly recommend CAREER MAPPING to anyone for whom professional growth is a high priority."

Kevin M. Kermes
FOUNDER, ALL THINGS CAREER

"For less than a Starbucks coffee, and a little motivation, I ended up with a career map and the knowledge to keep it refreshed! It takes a true expert to boil various concepts down to the core and make them usable. Dorothy clearly knows her stuff and it paid off for me and I am sure it will for you, too."

Eric Freitag
AMAZON REVIEWER

CAREER MAPPING

*Planning
your career
on purpose*

Get Free Instant Access to Video series,

"The 5 Most Common Ways Introverts Commit Career Self-Sabotage and How to Avoid Them"

These videos are designed to accelerate your results
with **CAREER MAPPING,**
and are my way of saying "thank you" for purchasing this book.

www.introvertwhisperer.com/career goals

Contents

THE INTROVERT
WHISPERER™

CAREER
MAPPING

*Planning
Your
Career
on Purpose*

DOROTHY TANNAHILL-MORAN

CHAPTER 1

Introduction to Career Mapping for Climbing Managers

YOU HAVE TAKEN A great step toward planning a management career you want to have. I speak to people every day who are dissatisfied with their career or job and are searching for how to get on a track they will enjoy. I truly believe a very big part of their issues stem from a lack of clarity and direction. People who are clear about what they want and where they are headed tend to focus on those activities that will support their goals.

Things like a bad boss or dysfunctional environment, of course, do create problems. However, your ability to gauge those things early and have a willingness to correct your situation are easier when you are clear about what you need out of each experience.

This is also not your usual self-help book with loads of fluff and repetition. This is the no-kidding,down-to-earth information and direction you will want to use to take action planning your future. It's the very same process I have used for myself and my clients for years.

Lastly, I have one thing for you to keep in mind.

It's not "just" a job; it's half your life. Love your career.

CHAPTER 2

Overview—
Planning Your Career On Purpose

Y OUR CAREER CAN EITHER happen to you or you can make it happen. The thing we know for sure is that it won't stay the same, nor will you.

Way too many people really don't like their job or career. Depending on what survey you read, the number can be a staggering sixty percent of us don't like what we're doing. That is way too much time spent unhappy, especially when you consider that, other than sleeping, you will spend more time working than anything else you do inlife.

It's not JUST a job—it's half your life. It's time for you to love your career so you can lead a completely fulfilling life.

I believe that a big contributor to the dissatisfaction that comes along with our careers is the fact that we put very little planning and thought into where we're going. This is especially true as a growing and climbing manager. You have to know where you're headed so you can also direct your organization. The saying: "If you don't plan where you're going, that's where you'll end up," seems to apply to our career. You need to define where you are going and how you will get there—just like a car trip. That's why I refer to this process as a career map.

Just like planning a road trip, you put thought, research, planning and validation into your plan. You don't just jump in the car and start driving. You have to know where you are headed, how you will get there and how long it will take. You must provision your trip with gas, oil and maps. Because you want to enjoy both the journey and the destination, you want to know what you can do between point A and point B. But, most people put more time, energy and thought into planning a vacation than they do their career. You put this kind of time into your vacation planning so you will thoroughly enjoy yourself. Imagine how great things would be if you put that kind of thinking into your career . . .

Let's get real for a minute. Most people think of "planning" as boring, tedious and a waste of time. Not an appealing or alluring activity.

What if your career map held the same kind of excitement as planning a vacation? It's time to hit the reset button on your attitude for planning your life and career. This is about you! How much more exciting can it get? Besides, this process is going to build in your vision for your career; and the great thing about a vision is it will get you excited.

The process you are embarking on will be easy to follow. This process is straightforward to do and will give you all the steps and actions you need to take. It is practical and relevant to your specific situation and not some "pie in the sky" process that sounds good but doesn't really work.

Not only that, but as you move forward, you can continue to reuse this process repeatedly throughout your career. You are building a vital skill that will serve you as long as you work.

I might also point out that as a manager this is a superb process to use with the people who report to you. They will feel like they are nurtured and matter to youand the company. Imagine the productivity when each person translates their growth goals into daily action!

Because it's always good to know where you're going and why, let's look at the steps in your career map.

1. **Create Your Career Vision.**

   PURPOSE: One of the things that charges your batteries is a vision of your career that really excites you. This is you thinking about the big picture of what's possible, if not a bit scary because it is so audacious.

2. **Define Your Short-Term and Long-Term goals.**

   PURPOSE: Think of this as figuring out how long it will take you to get from one point to the next. Just like your road trip, you will think through how long it will take for you to get to various points as well, and which order things need to happen. As part of your goals, we look at such things as how to position yourself for growth and promotion.

3. **Execute A Gap Analysis.**

   PURPOSE: As you look forward to your next career step, you have to analyze what resources, skills and experience you need to get there. This is your "provisioning" step, like putting gas and oil in your car.

4. **Create Your Short & Long-Term Goals.**

   PURPOSE: Your plan only works if you identify specific actions you should take and when you will take them. This helps keep you accountable to yourself to ensure you don't "go to sleep at the wheel."

5. **Validate Your Plan.**

   PURPOSE: You need buy in to your plan with your management in order to get their support and potential opportunities. You need to make sure that your plan, and the actions you take, are ones that matter, not just to you, but also to the decision makers.

6. **Build Accountability Structures.**

   PURPOSE: All the planning in the world won't make any difference if you do nothing. You need to put structures in place to help ensure you do what you intend.

"If you limit your choices only
to what seems possible or reasonable,
you disconnect yourself from what you truly want,
and all that is left is a compromise."

ROBERT FRITZ

"Cherish your visions and your dreams
as they are the children of your soul,
the blueprints of your ultimate achievements."

NAPOLEON HILL

CHAPTER 3

Creating Your Career Vision

I OFTEN THINK IT'S important to define things, as it distills down our understanding of something to its most basic form. It helps us get on the same page. I think the idea of creating a career, much less any vision, is a foreign concept to many people. It may feel too "woo-woo" or abstract and, therefore, of limited value. I hope to dispel any resistance you might have for doing this first and important step.

Webster defines vision as: a vivid picture created by the

imagination; to picture oneself.

My own definition: A mental image that personally defines and inspires a person to take action toward a picture of their actual life. If it is powerful, it creates a personal desire to bring that image to reality. A vision provides a direction and meaning.

What Makes A Career Vision Important?

You need to create a gravitational pull for yourself toward your career goals. Anything truly great starts with a strong, clear vision of what you can look forward to. It is your reason for doing what you are doing.

As you probably know by now, many people embark on things in their life and career and quickly lose focus. It's hard to stay focused on so many important things going on in your life. We tend to drop our attention on those things that really aren't that resonant or compelling.

Quick story to make my point:

I had a friend who started planning for early retirement and what she would do with her free time. She made a list of activities and I quickly noticed that she was mostly describing activities like organizing her things using tubs and labels. When I asked her about her retirement plan, she confessed it didn't really excite her too much. I asked her just how excited she was over organizing things in plastic tubs, and if that is how she wanted to define this next milestone of her life. After she quit laughing, she realized that she lacked a vision and had simply created a "things to do list."

There is a saying: *"There are two important days in your life. The day you were born and the day you figured out why."*

You need to understand what is important to you in your career and the direction you want it to take. The inspiration you have for your vision will be the fuel for your journey. It will help you stay focused and clear about why you are setting out to do the things you will be doing. As a manager, this step should be particularly potent, as you have at your disposal the ability to inspire and positively impact those who work for you.

A vision for your career is vital, as it will be the inspiration that sustains you over the course of time. Your vision is the light at the end of a dark tunnel when things aren't going right to remind you why you are doing what you're doing. Your vision becomes your personal yardstick to help you measure the importance of what you are doing and to help give you focus.

Can Or Should Your Career Vision Change Over Time?

One of the misconceptions we have about our goals and vision for things is that it shouldn't change if it's really a good vision in the first place. While I do think a true, exciting vision doesn't change very quickly, it can change as life and circumstance mold our view or values.

Quick story to make my point:

A high placed manager in a big Fortune 500 company had a vision of one day making it to VP status and enter into the company's executive staff. This vision held in place through years and multiple promotions until she was on the highest level just before making it to the VP level. Once she got there, the vision she had of VP status and executive staff disappeared. While she loved the journey that got her there, she better understood the job content and culture of that next level.

Based on what she had discovered, as well as her own changing values, she realized another direction was better suited for her. When I asked her about her change of vision, she said: "I realized that what I really wanted, I had already accomplished. I also realized I probably wouldn't enjoy that next level as much as I had enjoyed where I'd been. It was time for a new vision." The vision she had initially created sustained her for years—in fact a decade; and now it was time to change.

We do see some people who have created a vision for their future as early as their teen years that never swerves or wavers. That is a rare person. For the rest of us mere mortals, we change our minds.

There is no guideline for how frequently a career vision might change, but let me suggest some things for you to consider:

A career vision doesn't change because you meet with

failure or challenge. You will meet with failures and problems along the way. If you change your vision every time this happens, you really don't have a resonant vision or you give up too easily. You will not have a sense of any real accomplishment because your vision continuously shifts as you meet with challenges. You need to toughen up.

A job is not a career. If your job doesn't support your goals or values, you need to move on. Just because moving from your job is tough doesn't mean it's a bad idea. Don't hang on to a job if it isn't serving you well.

You need to make real progress toward your vision before changing your vision. If you have a great vision for your career, you need to allow enough time to hit some of your milestones. We tend to be impatient and your career is not something you can be impatient with. There may be action plans you change as you progress (and that makes sense as you will learn later) but not your vision.

How Do You Create A Vision?
Good question. Creating a vision isn't like an academic exercise. It's turning inward, asking questions and answering them as much from the heart as from the head. It may take a few times doing these exercises before you have set yourself free enough to allow your imagination to take hold.

Your vision doesn't include elements of time or actions. It should act as a beacon to help direct you over time. It may have characteristics of bigness or greatness that you truly aspire for. That's okay to admit that you have those desires because this is your vision, there is no right or wrong to it, nor is there anyone to pass judgment on it. You are free to define whatever you want.

At the heart of your vision is an expression of your values—the things that are truly important to you. When we recognize our most important values and find a vision that honors them, we have created the spark for lasting personal inspiration.

Quick story to make my point:

This story is about me and my vision as a life and career coach. My vision was be the catalyst to help people see what is possible in their careers. To provide the information, teaching, insight and coaching to make that possible. I have had several great careers and know just how it affects all the other parts of my life, yet I see too many people who simply don't have that experience. Knowing that it's possible for everyone to love their career/work drives me each and every day. I created that vision over four years ago and it's as alive and motivating to me today as it was then.

Exercise: Read through the following questions to familiarize yourself with the questions. Then find a comfortable place to sit where you can relax as well as write.

We will start with three warm up questions. Ask yourself each question, one at a time. Then sit back in your chair, close your eyes and begin visualizing your response. When you are done, record your response/visualization.

1. What is important to you in your career?

2. What do you want from your career? How will that impact your life?

3. What would an ideal day look like? What kind of things would you be doing?

Now, let's move to the bigger, more daring questions about your career. Start by reading the question first then sit back in your chair, close your eyes and ask yourself the question. Start visualizing your answer.

Within the vision you have, explore it completely. Think about how it makes you feel. Examine the types of things you are doing and the kind of people who are working with you. Think about the type of position you are performing and determine what you like about it.

In other words, you really want to spend time understanding your vision using all of your senses and imagination. Record what you have seen.

1. If you could do or be in any career what would it be?

2. What kind of legacy do you want to leave?

3. What do you want to be known for?

4. What makes a career in management important to you?

5. At your retirement party, what kinds of things do you want people to say about the work you have done, impact you have made and the highest level of achievement you have attained?

As you can see, these are big questions that are worthy of your time and thought. The more thought and writing you can put into this visioning, the better. You will also notice that your vision might be lofty and even somewhat undefined in terms of career specifics. A vision can range from owning a business to a way you want to be or values you want to uphold.

Take It Up A Notch

We all learn and communicate in different ways. This means that for some people doing this vision work it's not yet "real" for you or that perhaps you need some additional elements to give you the boost you need.

Creating a Vision Board may be just the thing you need to take your vision from your head and paper into a visual mode to reinforce it for you. As well, when we see representations of our dreams, it acts as an ongoing "ping" to your brain about what you are going after. It will help keep your vision in front of you.

A vision board is simply a compilation of pictures, images, words and elements that reflect what exists for you inside your vision. You can prepare a vision board by going to a craft store to purchase a poster board, glue and colored pens. From there, you can search magazines or the internet for images that signify various elements of your dream. Perhaps it will be what your office or place of business looks like. It could be some of the work you will perform or who you work with. It could be an image of a large audience applauding you for a profound speech you have given or even a product launch like Steven Jobs.

If you are more technically oriented, you can use various computer graphic tools to create your vision board. Don't be limited by any medium to create something that will work for you.

Two quick stories to make my point:

In the video of *The Secret,* John Assaraf talks about his own vision board. He had packed it and had it stored for a while. Then after remodeling his new home, he opened the box the vision board was packed in. After telling his son about what a vision board was, he noticed that he had put a house on the vision board. He was now living in that very house.

My own similar story.

When I was a kid, I had found this snow white paper bag while staying with my Grandmother. It was perfect to draw a picture of a house. Forty years later when my mother shipped my childhood toys and possessions to me, I came across that picture I had drawn of a beautiful white, colonial home. It was the very home my husband and I had

> just built, even though I hadn't seen that picture or remembered it all those years. The power of your vision will help drive you to produce those very results.

Again, this vision board is for you, so you can put on it anything that reminds you of what you are pursuing. You can add your own words to enhance it. You may discover that you continue to add to it as time goes by to keep it fresh and live in your thoughts.

Now What?

Once you have gone through a visioning exercise, it usually feels too big and too exciting to hide it away from the world. In fact, it shouldn't be kept to yourself. You should share it because there are several good reasons it helps you in the longrun.

1. You should share it, as speaking it out loud is another way to reinforce the vision and to make it real.

2. By sharing it, others support you, which increases the power of your vision. It further empowers you.

3. Inspiration is contagious. You can be the catalyst for others to explore their own potential and to create their own compelling vision with your support.

There is one note of caution regarding with whom to share your vision. You want to be fairly selective in choosing those people. We all have well-meaning friends and relatives who will give you the countless reasons why your vision won't work or that it will cost you or take you a long time to get there. You don't need to hear that kind of feedback nor do you need someone who will be critical or judgmental—not for your vision. A vision doesn't need approval, nor does it need to be to be scrutinized in any way.

When you seek others out to share your vision with, you are looking for someone who isn't there to pass judgment, advise you or critique what you are sharing.

Once you have identified who you think you will share this vision with, it is best to prepare this person to be in the correct frame of mind. Let them know this is important to you and you would like them to listen, ask questions to clarify and to cheer you on. You might also want to consider asking them to help you stay accountable to your vision in the years to come. You could make this an annual event.

You might feel compelled to ask for feedback since we are so well trained to ask for it at work. If you do want to ask for feedback, ask if they have a sense from you of excitement and commitment. Avoid asking if it's good or worthy, as you are really the only person to know the answer. By asking about your energy as you have expressed your vision to them, it is a good reading of whether or not this is a truly resonant vision that will continue to inspire you over time.

An example of this is the woman I previously mentioned who had a list of things to do rather than an inspired vision of her future. It wasn't resonant for her and it was obvious to me that she wasn't that excited when she talked about it.

You also want to think through where or when you share your vision. You don't want to be interrupted or have distractions. A disruptive environment won't help the other person get a reading from you on your energy or resonance for your vision. You won't get the other person's undivided attention, which means they won't be at their best for this activity. Pick your time and location carefully so you get the most out of it.

If you have completed and documented your vision either in writing or vision board (or both) you have done well. You are ready to move on to the next step of creating your short-term and long-term goals.

CHAPTER 4

Goals: Long Term vs Short Term

GOALS ARE ONE of our greatest tools for accomplishing things, as well as driving us forward. However, there are a number of things that we tend to do to undermine our efforts and leave us less-than-impressed with the goals we take. We're going to turn that around for you in this section so you know how to construct a goal that will set you up for success and keep you focused.

As a manager that is responsible for the work and setting

direction of others, this type of planning is key to your success within the business. If you have not done this level of planning for your group, I suggest you use this Career Map to do the group planning.

Please note that your plan should bear a relationship to your group plan, but they are two separate plans. You will want to ensure you are planning those things that will make the biggest impact toward getting you to the next level. Now that you are a manager, that means "with and through your people." Your growth plan will have things in it that you will do on your own in addition to group accomplishments.

Milestones Versus Goals

You will notice in this next section that I refer to goals and milestones. I want to strive for simplicity as I previously mentioned. I will use the term "goal" and "milestone" interchangeably, as they both are defined so similarly. I'm sure there are some people out there that might go crazy with this, but my goal is simplicity and ease of execution. There is just no rationale for any further refinement in terminology.

We are going to look at your career goals in two windows of time. The first window will actually be short-term, which for this definition will be one year. The second window will be between two to three years or said another way: beyond twelve months. I'd like to explain my rationale for the windows and their length.

Short-Term or One-Year Window:

A one-year window for goals is a very do-able practical period of time. In one year you can accomplish quite a few of things in relationship to your bigger, longer-term career goal.

Because it is so short term, it's easier to "see" the things you need to do and can take action on.

There may be portions of your plan that require some actions to be sequenced, like taking a series of classes where some of those classes can be enrolled and executed on in the next couple of quarters, but perhaps not all completed for a couple of years.

Another way to look at a short-term goal is that it is like a stepping-stone that will get you to another step or to your destination. The thing you want to be mindful of with your short-term goals is the tendency to overload yourself with too many actions thus overwhelming yourself in the process. You risk derailing yourself once you become overwhelmed with too many things to do.

Quick l to make my point:

A woman I life-coached was very good at continuously making goals for all aspects of her life. These goals ranged from her health and relationships to projects she wanted to do. She was also a person prone to stress, which in turn negatively impacted her health. Her goals were so numerous that they would take up the better

> part of one page, single-spaced. It was apparent that most of the stress she experienced was of her own making because she was overwhelming herself with too many goals.

She was doing what I call "trying to eat the elephant." You simply can't try to do everything you want to do all at once. By prioritizing the most critical things, or eating the elephant in bite-sized pieces, you can avoid stress and be your best at executing the things that are really the most important.

For your short-term goals, you want to ensure that you are clear about what actions and results will move you toward your bigger career goal. If you don't truly know, then part of your work to formulate your plan will be to do your homework by speaking to people and researching. I'll spend some more time on this later, as it is an important step.

Quick story to make my point:

When I had decided I wanted to be a coach, I set out to put together both my short-term and long-term goals. My research into the profession led me to multiple conversations with people who were already in the coaching field as well as online research. From there, I spent time looking at and investigating various coaching schools.

From the research I gathered, I was able to lay out

my first year plan in specific detail. I also knew some things I would need to do the following year that would get me to a fully qualified coach with a business website. I also continued to add to both short-term and long-term plans as I learned more and accomplished my milestones.

While it may be possible that by the actions you take, you will get yourself to your bigger career goal in this one-year window, generally that is not the case. If it is your situation, I'll guide you on what to do for your long-term window goals.

Your Long-Term or Two to Three Year Window:
You may have a vision for yourself that could take longer than two or three years to accomplish. There is a difference between your goals and your vision. When you accomplish your long-term goal, it may or may not be your vision. It may be another stepping stone to your vision, which means that your career planning should be an ongoing process.

In fact, depending on your vision, you may be in a continuous state of striving towards it as it may be more of a state of being (like my vision of helping people see what's possible and loving their career) or a specific position (like when I wanted to be a manager at a specific level.)

When I worked for my previous employer, they were very good at planning and in fact had an annual period where they would plan five years out in time. I came to understand several things about that size of a planning window.

The first thing was that for the massive land purchases and multi-million dollar custom equipment needed for manufacturing, that kind of advanced planning was necessary. The second thing I learned, was that other than those things, that window was simply too big to plan for.

For things like human resources, marketing and sales, trying to plan that far out made almost no sense. The investment for those types of groups was not as massive and for the work that was done, the window to plan and execute was much shorter. The conditions that drove those groups, therefore the people, process and equipment was different, making a shorter window more valid for planning purposes. A bigger or longer window was impractical because the things that would drive change and response to it were different and didn't take five years to respond to.

The same is true for your career. Our career path is usually never completely straight. It zigzags its way forward as different opportunities present themselves; and our life circumstances can impact it. We will frustrate our efforts if we don't allow for a certain amount of response to our own environment. In other words, the longer the window for planning your future, the more likely it will change dramatically. That degree of change won't help you in the long run. It will simply eat up your time unnecessarily.

Another observation I have made is that for most "corporate" jobs, and even those not classically corporate, many career milestones come in two to three year windows. This is especially true in the earlier portions of your career. Promotions and opportunities, as well as positions, are more plentiful at lower levels.

That does tend to slow down as you have achieved higher management levels. Even at the higher-level positions, most people still clamor for growth and new stimulation, which means that at about the two to three year mile marker, you're ready for a change, although it may not be a promotion.

The last argument on this definition for "Long Term" is that our own ability to know exactly what actions to take start getting fuzzier as you go out in time. Part of the reason for this is that you often don't know what you don't know until you amass more experience, knowledge and insight. In fact, you may have a placeholder for figuring out your next step once you get to a specific milestone.

Quick story to make my point:

Although I knew the path to launching myself as a coach and the basics for setting up my business, there were many things out in time that I didn't know how to plan for.

I knew I would have a website, but didn't know what it would contain. I knew that as time went

> by, I would figure out what it needed to contain, as
> I grew more familiar with coaching as a business.
> My plan allowed for a period of time to define and
> develop the content.

The same point is true today. I don't know exactly what my milestones will be for next year. I do know that some of the things I'm doing this year will allow me to promote certain services next year when I've fully developed them. The specifics of the promotions, timing and sequence will unfold over this year. Once I know those things, I can update my plan.

With a long-term goal, like everything out in the future, the further out in time you go, the less detail and fewer things you will define. That's okay. It will be your actions this year that will lead you to those long-term goals. As you will learn later, you will continuously be adding to your short-term goals and may also start more clearly defining your long-term goals.

Your career planning is an ongoing window. You will have things you are working on today or next month that may be accomplished in the next month or even week. Those get checked off so you can start working on the next item. As things get done in the front part of your plan, other things will get added.

To Summarize The Concepts:
SHORT TERM: Short term is actions and results you will accomplish in the next twelve months. Short-term

goals are more detailed and specific.

Short-term goals lead you to other long-term goals or career milestones.

LONG TERM: Long-term goals may be a combination of specific actions or placeholders for actions that require more definition.

Some actions outlined in your goals may need to be sequenced in a logical manner such as classes or projects.

Long-term goals are those goals that are beyond the one year window.

Long-term goals may evolve and become more detailed as time and more knowledge are accumulated.

Career planning is an ongoing process.

CHAPTER 5

Short-Term and S.M.A.R.T. Goal Creation

A KEY CONCEPT IN making goals that is worthwhile and helpful to your personal planning is known as SMART Goals.

SMART is an acronym for the characteristics of a well-structured goal. You want a goal that is do-able and meaningful for both the actions you are taking and the results you are striving to achieve.

How many times have we written down a goal to come back to it in several months, only to discover that what we were doing had no resemblance to what we wrote or that what we wrote doesn't make sense?

To avoid those issues, follow this structure for your career goals.

S = SPECIFIC. In order to have a goal that you can achieve, you have to be specific about what you want to get done. I have found that no matter if you are looking for a job or fitness changes, if you can't be specific, you probably won't accomplish anything.

Let me give you an example of "specific":

EXAMPLE #1:
I want to be healthy

— or —

EXAMPLE #2:
I want to lose ten pounds.

Big difference don't you think? When I hear people say they want to be "healthy", I always ask them what (specifically) does that mean? If you can't answer that question, then you don't have a good, specific goal that will cause you to take the right action. "Healthy" might be defined a hundred different ways making it too vague to be a good goal.

Clarity and specificity may be the hardest part of the

work you will do on your career planning. Answering the question "What do I want to be when I grow up?" is one of the toughest questions we face. Certainly, your career planning is part of that question. This requires your thought (which shouldn't hurt) and maybe some research.

M = MEASURABLE. If you can't actually measure your progress and know what you will accomplish, again, you probably won't. The example above is very measurable.

You may have goals that you think can't be measured. You have to be thinking of the outcome. Let's say your goal was to reduce your stress. To measure the reduction, you might give yourself a scale of 1 to 10. Your goal is to reduce your stress for month-end close from a ten to a five. Since it is your scale, you can define it, because it is relevant to what's important to your experience.

A quick story to make my point:

I often hear people who have what I would call "response" careers, like administrative assistants or customer service agents who believe that their performance can't be measured. This is because the nature of the job is to simply respond to others' demands. Yet, I contend that there is a yard stick (or measure) for everything.

Certainly, those around you are judging you, whether or not that is their intent. How do they measure you? They measure you on things like how quickly you deliver, your accuracy or your demeanor. You can translate that same thinking to your goals. If you can't measure it, it probably isn't a goal. If you want to learn a new software program in order to further qualify you for your next career step, then perhaps your measure of success for the goal is twofold: 1- you completed the class and 2- you were able to produce xyz report using the software.

Your measure is both that you learned something (took the class) and you also could apply or demonstrate your skill.

A = ACHIEVABLE. Sometimes people identify goals that are unrealistic and unachievable for a variety of reasons. You have to do a sanity check; and if you think you can't objectively figure this out, ask someone. If you have identified a goal that isn't realistic, you are setting yourself up for goal failure. Examples that come to mind are those silly goals you often hear at beauty pageants like: "Solve world peace." Are you kidding me?

As you ponder the question of achievability, you have to think about each specific goal you develop and ALL of the goals you are outlining. If you take on too many goals, you risk overwhelming yourself, which can lead to goal failure.

Things to consider for being achievable:

- Can you largely control the outcome or results?

- Is there any history with you or others

that suggest what you've taken for a goal is reasonable?

- Is the goal too big?

- Do you have too many goals?

- Do you have other things going on that will make achieving this goal a risk?

A quick story to make my point:

Many times when clients come to me to work on their career decisions, they are already impatient and want an answer now!

Because defining a timeframe for a personal epiphany is impossible to predict, I coach those clients to make a goal of completing the program in "X" months. We can control the work to be done, which makes that goal achievable, but if we said something like "Identify my new career in three months" it might be unrealistic, because you can't predict if that will happen.

Remember, goal setting is a planning activity. That means that you have to think about the totality of what you are planning for, as well as each individual goal.

The point of your goal setting is that you feel you are making progress by setting most goals so you can attain them. The bar for your "high jump" is where YOU put it.

R = RESONANT. Your goal has got to be something that gets you excited and interested. You don't want to take on goals for someone else nor do you want to have a goal that you really don't care that much about achieving. You risk goal failure if you do.

Another way to describe resonance is desire or motivation. If you aren't motivated towards the achievement of something, you probably won't do it. This is an important thing, if not the most important thing, to recognize about goal setting. The reason most people don't accomplish their goals is that they aren't really motivated.

The goal might be a good idea, but the world is full of good ideas that people do nothing about.

A quick story to make my point:

One goal I took for a few years was to learn to play golf. I kept doing nothing and rolling it forward to the next year. After doing that a few times, I sat back and examined what was going on. I really didn't care to learn to play golf, because I wasn't that interested in it. It possessed characteristics that didn't appeal to me, such as taking so much time out of a given day. I did want to do it to have something to do with my husband. I scratched it off my list. It wasn't resonant. It was a good idea, but it held no juice for me. I found other things we could both enjoy.

Another fallacy that some people fall in to is mistaking action for meaningful results. Doing something just for the sake of doing it isn't meaningful for goal achievement.

You are looking for results with your goals. It's the only thing that really matters.

T = TIMED. A timed goal is one that has a date or timing for the goal to be accomplished. As a coach, I'm constantly asking my clients "when will that be done?"

A great way you can stay accountable is to know when to achieve your goal. If your goal can be finished at any time, there is no motivation to start. If you don't start, you never finish. It's just that simple.

If we go back to the original goal of losing ten pounds, it is really incomplete. While it was specific and measurable, it was missing the important element of time. If we left time out of this, you could lose ten pounds this month or this year.

Your work effort to accomplish that goal might be very different based on just this one element in your goal setting. A better way of saying that same goal would be: *I will lose ten pounds by July 1 of this year.* Assuming that is achievable and resonant, that is a well-constructed goal.

Let's now look at some good and bad examples based on our SMART goal criteria:

EXAMPLE:
I will apply for twenty jobs every week. *Good*

Specific = it's about applying for jobs

Measurable = twenty applications

Achievable = about the actions that would lead to a new job rather than starting a new job which you can't control

Resonant = making systematic progress toward finding a job

Timed = every week

EXAMPLE:

In order to become a certified instructor, I will score eighty percent three times before the end of January 20xx on the M.E. exam. *Good*

Specific = scoring a specific level on a specific exam.

Measurable = scoring level.

Achievable = It is possible to score eighty percent as required, if I study.

Resonant = I'm excited to get certified as soon as possible.

Timed = by January 20xx

EXAMPLE:

I will write a book. *Not good*

This isn't specific, or measurable, nor time bounded. A better goal is to have a book outline done by a specific time in the event that you don't have enough detail.

EXAMPLE:

I will finish reading the M.E. theory manual and pass the theory exam by February 15, 20xx. *Good*

EXAMPLE:

I will get certified as a M.E. trainer. *Not good*

While this one does have the specifics of being certified and measurable in order to become a trainer, it's missing the time element.

EXAMPLE:

I will have fun this summer. *Not good*

This doesn't define anything other than a timeframe.

EXAMPLE:

I will have fun by hosting two to three guests visit and tour Savannah Georgia this summer. *Good*

This goal takes the concept of having fun this summer and gets specific in terms of activities, measurable because you have identified all of the minimum conditions and is time bounded insomuch as it defines the timeframe. This is an example of goal setting something that could potentially be kind of mushy for a goal.

CHAPTER 6

Long-Term Goals and Goal-Setting Work

Y OU NOW HAVE ALL the basics for creating your career goals, so it's time to get to work.

For this exercise, make a chart named **LONG-TERM GOALS** with 3 columns labeled: **A–Goal Milestone**, **B–Target Due Date**, and **C–Results** or **How to Measure when Achieved**.

A	B	C
Goal Milestone	Target Due Date	Results or How to Measure When Achieved

With your vision in mind, the next big question for you to consider is: What career milestone do you intend to accomplish in the two to three year timeframe? Insert this in Column A.

Once you know your milestone, you need to determine your timeframe. Enter the due date in Column B.

Next, determine how you will know you have achieved this (these) goal. I.e.: What evidence, results must be in place for you to concretely say you have achieved this? (Keep in mind measurable and resonant.) Insert your results in Column C.

What To Do When You Don't Know Enough.

As mentioned, you will not have much detail for the goals the more you go out in time. You will also come to understand that there will be things you need to research before you know your specific actions. Since this is a planning tool, you may want to outline a goal for doing the research that will inform you on other steps you need to take. This can still have the characteristics of SMART Goals and once you move through that goal, it will inform you with much more detail that you can add to your short-term or even long-term goal.

Recall a previous quick story:

Earlier I mentioned my path to becoming a coach. I knew only the briefest of long-term goals like I wanted to be certified as a coach and launch a business and website. In order for me to define my short-term goals, I took a goal of researching what it would take to become a coach. Once that was accomplished, I had specifics that allowed me to add great detail to my short-term goals and a few to my long-term goals.

What To Do When Your "Big" Goal Is Accomplished This Year.

It is entirely possible that your next career milestone could be accomplished this year. If that is the case, you still need to be thinking about your "What next?" question. If you foresee a series of promotions, then that would be your long-term goal, even if it might be on the outer limits of the two to three year window. That's okay because you do always want to be thinking about where you are headed.

I want to point out a reaction we often get once you achieve a career milestone, such as a promotion. The reaction we tend to have is to "focus on now and not focus on the future." We feel like taking a breather for a while and stop running the race quite so hard. It's understandable, because you should enjoy the spoils of your effort. You may feel like you don't need to define your goals for a while. The caution on taking a break from your career goals is that you once again could get swept up in simply working and not paying attention to where you're headed.

A better suggestion is to take short-term goals around your own new job integration and learning curve followed by a placeholder for a date out in time to figure out your next long and short-term goals. This will keep you focused on your career, even if you aren't overly active for a period of several months.

CHAPTER 7

Short-Term Goal Setting

NOW THAT YOU'VE laid out your long-term goals, you are well positioned to define your short-term goals. These will be the actions you will pursue over the course of the next twelve months, updated quarterly.

For this exercise, make a chart named **SHORT-TERM GOALS** with three columns labeled: **A-Goal Milestone**, **B-Target Due Date**, and **C- Results** or **How to Measure when Achieved.**

A	B	C
Goal Milestone	Target Due Date	Results or How to Measure When Achieved

With your long-term goals in mind, the next big question for you to consider is: What actions do you need to accomplish in the next twelve months that will either get you there, or will contribute significantly? Insert this goal in column A.

Enter the date you plan to complete this goal in Column B.

Next determine how you will know you have achieved this (these) goal, ie: What evidence, results must be in place for you to concretely say you have achieved this? (Again keep in mind measurable and resonant.) Enter this in Column C.

CHAPTER 8

Gap Analysis

G AP ANALYSIS IS MY OWN little term that I have attached to the activity of "figuring what's in the gap." This is particularly important if you are pursuing a promotion or a new career as your next career milestone. It is not enough to say you want to be promoted. You have to know in fairly specific terms, what you have to do to earn the promotion.

It's not enough to work hard and perform well. You need to understand the difference between where you are positioned today in terms of things like your skills, experience and behaviors and what those need to be at the next level. It's the information you derive by this analysis that will flow into your short-term goals.

Conducting this analysis requires work with your manager and perhaps other leadership in your company or industry. You will want to start the process by doing your own gap analysis; and to get promoted, the opinion of management is what will complete this work. At the end of the day, it's management that will assess you and should tell you what it takes to be promoted. It is the work you do with them that will give you the information you need to help you define your short-term goals.

How To Conduct A Gap Analysis:
The basic equation to a gap analysis is:

> Skills and experience as identified by you, mentors and/or your boss for your career goal position (subtract) your existing skills and experience (equals) those things you need to "fill the gap."

The first step you need to do is to fully understand where you may be deficient in your skills, education or experience for the career goal or position you want to pursue. This is an important step to take in the development of both your short-term and long-term goals.

Don't assume that by your own simple observation that you know what is required. You need to obtain direct input through conversations and study to supply you with a list of requirements.

A quick story to make my point:

When I was managing a group previously, I had a woman who came to me from another department who wanted a specific job in my group. She had done her homework of identifying her skills versus those for the position she wanted to ultimately compete for. She wanted me to validate that the skills she was about to work on were in fact, "necessary and sufficient" to do the targeted job. She not only had done her gap analysis and validated it with me, she impressed me immensely with the work she had done. Needless to say, when the time came, she got the job!

Following are the various steps you can take to obtain the information you need. I suggest you pursue at least three of these to validate a final list.

a. Acquire job descriptions for your desired positions that detail out the requirements and job responsibilities. Ideally, these should be from your current company. If none are readily available, ask HR or your management for copies of previous job descriptions.

b. Interview people currently doing the job or work associated with your goal. Get their insight on needed skills to do the job, as well as a profile of what skills they possessed when hired or promoted to that position.

c. Speak to a trusted mentor to get their input on both your current skills and the skills needed for your career goal/position. Ideally, this person should be at a level above yours so they can have a perspective that may be broader than your own.

d. Work with your boss to obtain an assessment of your skills and what they would like to see you do to move to the next level. Because you work for this person, you need to weight their input the heaviest, as their opinion of your promo ability will be the most critical.

e. Make sure where you are headed is a needed position. There should be a need you intend to fill. If not, there is no market for what you are pursuing. It may be in your existing company or elsewhere, but in either case, if there is very little demand, you may end up frustrating yourself later.

A quick story to make my point:

I speak to people on a regular basis that tell very similar stories about launching into a degree or taking classes as a means to get them to a long-term career goal—without doing the work necessary to know if their actions will matter.

One such person I spoke to was a very smart guy

who had been very successful selling insurance. He embarked on a degree as a means to change careers. The problem he ran in to was twofold: 1) he hadn't amassed any related experience which was critical to his new career, and 2) he lived in a small community that didn't have enough or the right kind of businesses where that career existed. It was like giving a Cadillac to a third-world citizen where no gas pumps existed. Might be nice to have, but had no practical application or use based on where he lived. A gap analysis would have given him a better set of actions to take.

If you receive discrepant or conflicting things, don't be discouraged. That can happen sometimes. If this should happen, you may want to identify those items and ask the people you worked with their opinion on the discrepancy. There are many paths to the same destination and certainly, this is true for careers. When you hear more than one opinion for how to get the needed skills and experience for your career goal, you will have to apply some judgment on what you will pursue and what you will drop or delay. You will also get more insight by following up on those items that you may have missed in your earlier reviews. You can never know too much.

The items you gather in this step should be in your short-term goals and depending on the nature of the item, may be in your long-term goals.

CHAPTER 9

Action Plan Validation

B Y THIS POINT, you have done your work to first identify your next career destination and conducted a gap analysis.

Before finalizing your short-term (and maybe your long-term) goals, you need to ensure you have validated your plan. The primary source for validating your plan should be with your current manager and perhaps the manager at the next level.

No matter how high your management position, you will always have someone who is the ultimate decision maker about what it takes to move to the next level.

It is their opinion of you that matters the most when a decision is made to promote you or give you that next assignment. All too many people simply believe that to work hard will get you to the next step. While hard work is important, if it's not hard work on the right things, it probably won't make a difference.

You have to remove as much guess work out of this process as you can. It's also vitally important to understand that while you may validate your plan with your management, it is not a guarantee of any future promise by your management. There are too many variables to make that kind of guarantee, but you reduce the likelihood of a misstep by taking this action. You will also find your management much more invested in your success if you engage them upfront and along the path to your next destination.

When you have completed your gap analysis and any follow up, summarize and prioritize the actions you will undertake. This summary is what you will want to review and validate with your management. It's highly likely that they will play an instrumental role in supporting your endeavors, as they may need to approve of some of the things you need to do. They may also need to assign you specific work to get your skills developed. Be prepared for some modification based on this discussion, but once you fully discuss and agree on your plan, update it and ensure you both have a copy.

A quick story to make my point:

I had an admin who longed to be a programmer. I was constantly being asked to pay for various classes that didn't relate to the position as an admin. Finally, I asked this person to explain to me either their career path or how the classes related to the job of an admin, as it wasn't clear to me what they were going to accomplish.

Once I understood the long-term career goal, I set up a three-way meeting with a person who did the type of work the admin was wanting to do. In the course of that meeting, we both learned that the classes being pursued would not achieve that goal. The classes were fun, but didn't apply to the current job much less to the overall career goal. It was an unhappy time for this person, but better to adjust sooner rather than after time and money were spent needlessly.

Following this discussion, take it upon yourself to periodically follow up with your management to check your progress and to get their input on your performance. You want to know if you need any performance corrections earlier rather than later.

Also, keep in mind that since this is your plan and your goals, it is your responsibility to keep this line of communication going. Again, you don't want to take needless action and be down the road a year to find out that your actions didn't matter or weren't really sufficient.

As I mentioned, their validation of your plan and ongoing guidance is not a guarantee of a promotion, but you will have greater support if you do. As well, if your actions are insufficient, you will learn this by ongoing communication.

Too many people get surprised; and my feeling on most of these is that they can be largely prevented by front-end agreements and ongoing dialogue.

CHAPTER 10

Accountability Structures

THERE ARE TWO weak points with the undertaking of any endeavor. The first one is simply getting started.

The second one is losing focus and sustaining inertia over a long period of time. Assuming you have read and started this process of mapping your career, you have overcome the first weak spot. The next thing for you to think about and plan for will be how to keep you going over a long period of time.

I'd like to share quickly a five-part change model that Dr. James Prochaska has outlined in his book *Changing For Good*. He has studied and tested this model over many years of his practice as Director of Cancer Prevention Research Center at the University of Rhode Island. It's unclear to me why the general public doesn't understand more about the skills and structures it takes to undergo a successful change effort. Even if we think we are resistant to change, that is simply an urban myth. We make changes continuously and will continue to until the day we die. There is a key element to this change model that people need to know so they increase the odds of being successful in any of their change efforts, be it losing weight or pursuing a career goal.

Here Are The Five Parts:

1. **PRE-CONTEMPLATION.** This is the stage where you don't yet really understand you have an issue to resolve or change. For people with dependencies to drug or alcohol, they may be in denial that they truly have an issue to fix. You are beyond that at this point, but if you think about your past, chances are there was a time you simply didn't give any thought to the direction your career was going. You were in this stage.

2. **CONTEMPLATION.** This is the stage where you recognize you have an issue, but are assessing if it

is worthy of your time and attention. For you, you may have thought you weren't particularly happy with your current job, but didn't yet have any clear thoughts about whether or not you would do something to change.

3. **PREPARATION.** This is the stage where you decide to move forward to make a change and address the concerns you have. During this stage you research your options and weight each one in terms of the way you think will best work for you. As with the steps I've mentioned previously, you might do internet research and speak to professionals to advise you. Again, you've done your homework and have pursued this material to help you to move forward.

4. **ACTION.** You now have your resources and steps identified and are in the active portion of your change. If you were losing weight, you would be dieting, exercising and perhaps seeking nutritional counseling, among other actions. For you, you are pursuing the steps I've mentioned above by creating your vision, identifying your short-term and long-term goals, gap analysis and meaningful research.

5. **MAINTENANCE AND ACCOUNTABILITY.** When you plan a change, you must plan for the potential collapse of your own momentum. It's a known statistic that only twenty to thirty percent of all people will be able to make and maintain a change on their own. With this step, the real work begins, although too many people think the action stage is "it." It's not. This is

the stage we will focus on in this section. It will be key to your success, not just in planning your career goals, but to achieve them.

What Is Accountability And How Do You Plan For It?

Accountability is where YOU are being held accountable for certain actions. In the workplace, there is what I call "built-in" accountability.

You have a boss and peers that hold you accountable to get done the work you have been assigned. When you don't, you either get fired or at least chastised. Punishment and the threat of unemployment are enough to keep most of us delivering what we should in the workplace. There are people in your midst that will help you remember these facts every day.

You could look at the previous statements a bit offensively, perhaps because you are responsible and professional. Keep in mind one thing I mentioned about stage/step five: "on your own." In other words, for sixty to seventy percent of people, they do need other people in the mix holding them accountable for most changes. While you might be in the minority at work, you may still be part of the statistics by not losing weight on your own or changing a habit you want to break. Even if you are very disciplined you still need to put these structures in place.

YOU PLAN YOUR ACCOUNTABILITY IN TWO PARTS:

Part 1. Give yourself specific dates to do things. While we've done most of the work on this part by ensuring your short-term goals have deliverable dates on them, there are additional things you can do that will help. I'll outline those shortly.

Part 2. Recruit people to help you stay accountable.

Let's examine Part 1 and look at the power of dates and the schedule. As I have said with the outline of S.M.A.R.T. goals, you need to identify a time or date you will have completed an action. Without that date, the goal could be completed at anytime or not at all.

The power of those dates becomes more dynamic for you if you now use your calendar to help you. If you already actively use a calendar, you know how valuable it is to have meetings scheduled. Those schedules ensure you meet with key people to help you move things forward, professionally and personally. If you don't actively use a calendar to manage any part of your time, now is the time to start.

If you use an electronic calendar, you may be able to use a feature to send yourself reminders about upcoming deliverables. With or without an electronic calendar with automated reminders, you do want to use your calendar with both a due date and an early warning reminder that a due date is coming.

A quick story to make my point:

I have depended on a calendar since I graduated from college. While it was a paper calendar then, I have converted to a computer-based calendar. The primary purpose of my calendar is to schedule appointments with clients as well as key people in my work and personal life. The other thing I use my calendar for is to input my various work milestones so there is no way I can ignore them. Depending on how much work is entailed I might also put in an "early warning" reminder in my calendar to remind me that I have to complete something by a certain date. I let my calendar help me stay accountable to my goals.

Another step for you to consider is to allocate time to work on a specific thing. At the beginning you may not know how long something will take for you to do. I suggest you allocate a minimum of 1.5-hour chunks of time in your calendar and certainly longer if you think it appropriate. I recommend over an hour because you will spend some time simply picking up the loose ends before you get into productive work time. If you haven't given yourself enough time, you may discover all you are doing is trying to figure out where you were when you left off and what your next step will be.

A quick story to make my point:

A friend and client of mine began writing a book. It was an important quest of hers as it was a commitment she had made to her sister who has passed away. Yet, as time went on I noticed that she was making minimal progress in her writing. After seeing this for a while, I suggested she literally set aside time on whatever schedule she needed to so she could write her book. It was important for her to take into account other obligations she had and for her to observe when the best time to write would be. With that in mind, she laid in a daily schedule on her calendar to write her book. From that point, her progress was amazing and she also discovered a renewed excitement because of the momentum she had created.

Scheduling her work time kept her accountable and moving at a pace that worked for her. It wasn't a drudge, but rather made her feel like she was really making progress. By the way, she finished her book in a matter of a few months.

It is all too easy to let our ongoing job and personal life distract us from our goals. When you set aside specific time to work on your career goals, you increase the likelihood that you will accomplish them and still have time for personal activities.

When Life Happens:
I'd also like to share a tip for really making this process work for you. Obviously, there will be occasions where circumstances dictate that you miss your scheduled work time for career goals. These tend to fall into two categories: 1) unexpected things, and 2) your loved ones want your time. There is a strategy for both situations.

For unexpected things: There will be things like getting sick, surprise tickets to a special event or unexpected deadlines. It happens. When you are in a situation that means you will "miss" your career goal work appointment—don't cancel it—reschedule it. In other words don't let that allocated time disappear altogether.

Review your schedule and reschedule your work time to a time that will work. Pay yourself back the missed time. Never let it slide. Be as professional about keeping your appointments with yourself as you would keep an appointment with a customer or your boss.

Your loved ones want your time: Other people may assume if you are home, you're game for great activity ideas. This problem happens sometimes to people who work from home. Depending on your situation, you may need to set boundary conditions with your friends and family to help support you in your effort. It can be as simple as setting aside a specific time each week that you declare as off boundaries. This lets others know that you can play, just not at that day and time. If you can't identify a consistent timeslot, consider going to a quiet space and indicate that when you're there, you'd prefer to be uninterrupted.

Quick story to make my point: The woman who wrote the book I mentioned earlier not only scheduled time to write, but she had to work out an agreement with her husband on her work space. She needed to use the family room to write. This meant if he wanted to watch TV, he needed to do so from another location in the home, when she was there and writing. She avoided relationship issues by working this ahead of time rather than kicking him out of the room each time he encroached on her space while working. It also helped her avoid picking up her things and moving when she really wasn't prepared to do so.

A SUPPORT TOOL:

Depending on your prowess with your calendar, or if you are the type of person that uses two alarms clocks in the morning, I have a tool suggestion to help you with your accountability. This is a free tool you can use without even going to the website each time to use it. It's called *Follow Up,* found at *www.followupthen.com.* What this will do is allow you to send email reminders to yourself or others at whatever time interval you choose. Obviously, this is a good tool in the workplace, as you will often send an email requesting something and never hear back.

This tool will allow you tosend the email and at the same time resend it to you both or just you to remind you of the request. It will also let you send reminders of things to yourself. This becomes a great tool for you to consider using to hold yourself accountable. Essentially, you can set up due date reminders and early warnings of due dates for all of the various goals you take.

I suggest you go to the website and listen to the two-minute video that will explain how to use it in a variety of ways. That's all it takes for you to start using it. You never have to return to the site again.

Build An Accountability Team:

You need help and you need support. This isn't a sign of weakness; it's a sign that you now fully understand that most people do need others to achieve most things that are worthwhile. We think we can go it alone and will have the fortitude to make most anything happen.

The statistics that I mentioned earlier prove that will not occur for the majority of people. Most likely that is you. I simply can't emphasize this enough. You need others to help you stay accountable to your career goals. One of the best approaches to involving others in keeping you accountable is to build a team of people. It is possible to have just one person acting as your accountability partner and I will make my suggestions if that is the route you take.

WHO IS THE RIGHT TYPE OF ACCOUNTABILITY PERSON?
You need to be thoughtful about the type of person and who that person might be. There are certain characteristics you should look for:

a. someone who will be serious about holding you accountable to meet your commitments

b. someone who will ask you the tough questions if you aren't on course

c. person who has some level of understanding about goals and how to make them specific

d. someone who is willing to tell you the hard truth as they see it, if the situation warrants it – and you will respect and listen to them when they do

e. you don't want someone who is a pushover and will simply go along with whatever you are saying, just to be nice to you

Some suggestions might be a co-worker or previous co-worker that you respected, worked well with and know can be the type of person you need. If you have considered a mentor at work, this would be a great time to secure that relationship. Mentors usually exist to help you move forward and one at work will know your situation and be great at giving you feedback.

Lastly, hiring a coach can help you achieve your career goals much quicker. The role of a coach is to help you define your direction and hold you accountable for getting there.

While it might seem like a good logical person might be your partner or spouse, more than likely that is a poor choice. We often create a set of dynamics with those closest to us that will not allow for the appropriate level of accountability or tough questions. We can get defensive, argue or just blow off their attempts to keep us true to our goals. It can create relationship issues if you aren't careful.

If you feel your relationship can shift in order to create this role, then certainly pursue it. Just know it is risky.

Team Versus Just One Person

The main advantages of having a team or more than one person holding you accountable is:

a. You get more than one perspective.

b. You may not have to demand as much time if you spread your follow up meeting over more than one person.

If you do have more than one person as your accountability partner, you don't need to meet with them together. Your meetings can be separate and at different times.

What Are You Asking Them To Do?

You are asking your accountability partners to meet with you on a regular basis for probably a few years. That may seem overwhelming at first, but you can also add socializing to those meetings. Since most relationships last for years, you really aren't asking for much more than what you may be doing already. If you are asking for more time, then it's best to be upfront with that information so this person can make a well-informed decision about your request.

In terms of frequency of meeting with your accountability partners, there is no perfect formula. You want to allow enough time to go by to ensure you have time to make progress. At the same time, you don't want so much time to go by that you lose momentum or you both lose a memory for the work to be done.

My personal suggestion is to consider every two months up to every three months at the most. Once you are in agreement, schedule your first meeting soon after simply to educate them on your plans. At the end of that meeting, agree on when you will meet again. DO NOT FAIL to schedule your next meeting while you are together. It's too easy to let it slip and both people forget.

You are asking them to hold you accountable to your career goals to ensure your success. You can review with them the list of attributes and confirm with them that they think they can fulfill your needs. While you may think they're able, they may not feel the same or feel completely comfortable with the responsibility. It's important that any response they give you when you make the request be okay. You don't want to be offended or defensive if they turn you down. It's vital that your relationship remain intact.

There you have it. If you have dates on your goals, goals with dates on your calendar and people to help you stay the course, you are well on your way to achieving all of your goals. That means you are well on your way to your dreams and your vision of what's possible for you in your management career.

Now What?

Keep in mind that your goals and this process are like a living organism. You should be working and accomplishing your short-term goals. You should be periodically moving your long-term goals into your short-term S.M.A.R.T. goals. You should once a year be identifying your next long-term goals.

It's an ongoing process if you let it be. As long as you are working, it pays to look ahead to get the most out of each thing you do. I also think that it's a good idea for you to be revisiting your vision to keep the feeling of it alive and vital for you.

Recognize that as time goes by our priorities and opportunities may change. That's okay. Don't let those changes make you think you were "wrong" previously. You have simply changed and change is core to our existence. When or if you should decide to change direction, you can start this process over again. You may discover that some parts of it are still resonant for you or maybe not. The point is you now have the skills, process and experience with this material to repeat it anytime in the future you choose.

Celebrate!

Don't be afraid to kick up your heels after accomplishing your various goals. All too often, we simply smile inside and move on. Self-recognition is as important as recognition from the workplace, peers or the boss. We don't self recognize as much as we should. Go out and buy yourself a cookie!

Thank you.

CHAPTER 11

Growth And Promotion

FOLLOWING ARE SEVEN articles I have written and published on the subject of how to get promoted and how to create career growth. I thought you might find this additional information and insight useful. Enjoy!

5 LEADERSHIP QUALITIES YOU CAN DEVELOP TO HELP YOU GET PROMOTED

REGARDLESS OF WHAT we call it—*Leadership, Managing, Being in charge, Supervising*—the fact is when we assemble more than one person, there is someone who is leading the effort. For many of us, that is the goal we pursue. For some of us it simply happens whether it's a goal we sought or not. The thing that is generally common is that in order to assume the role of a leader to people and their work efforts, there are traits that must be present in order to be effective.

Leadership qualities can seem illusive to some despite their desires or positions. Just because someone has been put in charge doesn't necessarily mean that those traits exist. I think that group we might call "bad bosses."

The good news is that you can develop those leadership traits even if they were not something you were born with. While attending management classes and reading books can all help, the best path to building those qualities is to observe great role models and exhibit those same behaviors.

Here are the leadership qualities that you can begin modeling today:

1. **Leaders don't hang back.** You will never notice a leader being half committed or reluctant to participate.

These people get quickly immersed into whatever the effort is, get knowledgeable and are generous with their skills and knowledge. This means you need to take an active role with the work your group is doing. Look for ways to contribute at a greater level. You may think your existing leader has to do something to "anoint" you with more. Don't wait: ask.

2. **Leaders take responsibility.** These people are willing to be responsible not only for their work but also for helping others to be successful. When things go wrong, they will step up and own their role and look to the future as an opportunity to improve. Be clear on what the expectations are and then go one step further.

3. **Leaders have initiative.** They don't wait for someone to figure out what to do. They look to see what needs to be done and do it. Words like self-starter come to mind. Can you imagine the president of the U.S. waiting to be told what to do? Look around your work area and find things that need improvement. Take it upon yourself to solve problems that will positively impact the business or create efficiency for your group. It won't go unnoticed.

4. **Leaders communicate openly and honestly.** Even leaders who are known to be introverts leave nothing to chance or guess. They communicate in various ways in all directions within their group. This trait, perhaps more than others, characterizes all great leaders, because it is within their communication that

they can lay out their vision to others. That clarity and consistency can unite people and cause them to lay down their life. The next time someone you admire speaks to you or your group, pay attention to what they say and how they say it. Check yourself for your reactions to what they say and what it is that causes that. There is a thought that you can't over communicate – start with that premise today.

5. **Leaders believe in what's possible.** You rarely hear a leader gripe or talk in depressed terms. They tend to think that they and others will succeed. Even in the face of defeat, they learn from it and move forward still with the belief that with enough drive, will and knowledge eventually they will prevail. This isn't being unrealistic; in fact, it's founded on good judgment. The secret that some people don't realize is that not starting, giving up and not seeing options usually create failure in business. Today you can start recreating a habit of how you view things. This may be the hardest thing to change or do differently, but positive attitudes truly are powerful.

If you're eager to be promoted or obtain more responsibility, keep these things in mind and add them to your personal brand. Over time, you will be "seen" as a leader and those opportunities will come your way.

6 WAYS TO ACHIEVE CAREER GROWTH

ALL TOO OFTEN WHEN the discussion about career growth rolls around, most people think in terms of promotion to management. While taking a management position can signify career growth, it isn't the only possibility.

Career growth is really all about your ability to learn new things and apply them. That learning curve, just like going to school, means you increase the depth and complexity of knowledge about your work. It is like the difference between grade school and high school.

Career growth is important to us all because as the pesky humans we are, we get bored easily; and boredom is created when there is nothing new to stimulate our thinking. Boredom can easily turn to job dissatisfaction, which should be avoided at all costs.

Here are some ways to create career growth:

1. **Take classes.** You may think since you graduated your brain is as full as it needs to be. Wrong. Now that you are in an actual work setting, you will discover many things to enhance how you do your work or to prepare you for the next step. There is a class for everything from computer applications to how to communicate more effectively.

2. **Ask for new assignments.** You might even suggest some tasks that you would like or that are in need of attention. Learning a new task expands your qualifications for doing new jobs.

3. **Become an expert.** All groups usually have a person who is the definitive expert at something. They spend time learning all they can about that one thing and when you ask them a question – they either know the answer or can get it better than any other person. As the "go-to" person your learning continues, because people will seek you out for help in solving the big, complex issues.

4. **Read.** You should be reading about your company regarding such things as the business direction, business results and market strategies. Knowing these things will give you an idea of where you fit. Also, reading is a good way to increase your learning; and just like classes, you can find a book that will apply to all situations and challenges you might be facing.

5. **Change jobs.** When you change jobs, you go through another learning curve; and that continues to expand your professional knowledge base. You also become more valuable because you've expanded your skills.

6. **Look for improvements.** All businesses have more challenges and work than they have manpower to tackle them. You can easily look around your own department and find many things you could work

on that would help the overall company. You need to ensure that what you are doing still allows you to perform all your assigned responsibilities. Pick out things that will cause you to learn something new in the process.

Career growth is primarily about expanding your knowledge and skills. When you are continuously increasing your capabilities, there is usually an offsetting reward of pay and promotion at some point. Even without those financial rewards you will feel better about yourself and your future.

ARTICLE #3:

I THOUGHT I WAS GOING SOMEWHERE! OR . . . WHERE IS MY PROMOTION?

YOU STARTED THIS JOB with bright eyes and full of promise. You were excited about the possibilities. You dreamed of sweet business victories capped off with promotions and huge paychecks.

You've now discovered you're still revving your engines at the starting line, same job with only the annual three percent pay increase. Oh boy. Your expectations are now turning to resentment and despair. This is not how you thought it would go.

This happens to a number of people every day and many of them simply succumb to apathy for years to come. You know the type; they are basically funky and unhappy, rationalizing where they are and where they are headed. Is this the new future for you or are you going to do something about it?

Assuming you would like to keep some of the dream alive, let's look at a variety of circumstances that may play into your situation, and then we'll look at some corrective action.

What may be contributing to a lack of growth or promotion?

- You may be waiting to have your brilliance

discovered like a starlet in Hollywood. The lack of self-promotion is a big problem for people. You have to get past the notion that good work will speak for itself. Think again. You don't have to be obnoxious to self promote; you simply need to make sure you've communicated to the key people what you have accomplished.

- You may not have made yourself clear. Does the boss know you want a promotion? To take on more responsibility? You don't have to set that expectation during your hiring interview, but at some point, you need to enlist the boss in your career aspirations to ensure support and opportunities.

- Are you going after it? Or waiting for it to come to you? Promotions won't fall into your lap. You have to go after the work at the next level while still performing superbly in your existing role.

- Did the business take a dive or shrink? If you survived a lay off while your company did the big shrink this past decade, the money and the opportunities probably went away. You may be doing all of the things mentioned so far and it absolutely made no difference. This may not have been your fault, but it is your responsibility to do something to get yourself growing again.

- You and the boss may truly be out-of-sync. You may be contributing some fantastic work and for all sorts of reasons it just doesn't turn the boss on. You are making no headway as long as this situation exists. You don't see it changing any time soon.

What can you do to correct the situation?

- Be clear about the direction you are headed and approximately when you want that to happen. Make sure you've counseled with your boss and any other key stakeholders to gain support and guidance.

- Seek out more than you're given. Show initiative and solve problems at or above your current level.

- Self promote. Not like a jerk, but communicate and engage all the key players in what you are doing and what you've accomplished.

- Move on. If the boss and/or the business situation are showing no signs of movement, it's time to find something else. We are hopeful creatures. Sometimes we're hopeful because we're too lazy to do a job search, hoping the boss will go or suddenly a major business windfall will occur. That is highly unlikely; so get to it before you turn into the cranky old person you are trying to avoid becoming.

Your promotions may have escaped you up to this point, but you can turn your situation around. Refuel your dream and get yourself back on track for great things.

ARTICLE #4:

CAREER PLANNING 101: MASTERING THE BASICS

ALL TOO OFTEN WE launch our careers simply by chance rather than by deliberate direction; and the direction we head after that looks very haphazard. While hard work and great results can definitely benefit your career trajectory, it still needs some consistent planning to really get the best results.

Even if you've been working for ages and never thought to do some career management for yourself, it's not too late to deploy some of these tactics to manage your career. If you are a newly minted graduate, you can fold these into your ongoing planning from day 1.

Tactics to manage your career:

Have a goal in mind. Even if you change your mind, continually be aiming at some specific career goal. It could be a promotion, advancement or an assignment to be pursued. By having a goal in mind, it helps shape your other actions. Without a goal, there's no telling where you will end up.

Get knowledgeable about the criteria for attaining your goal. Questions you should be continuously asking are: "What does it take to: - be promoted to the next level? – to receive advancement? – to be assigned to a juicy project?" This is like climbing a mountain. You first need to decide which mountain. Once you do that then you figure out the best way to get to your destination and what you need to support the climb.

Analyze your shortages. With your goal in mind, you need to turn your attention to what you need to equip yourself with in order to be qualified to attain your goal. There may be a skill you need to develop or up level, and if that is true, how will you accomplish it? You may need to enroll in a class or seek someone out to train you. It's safe to say that with all goals, there is action and knowledge required to get there.

Get insight. You would do well to speak to the people who have accomplished what you want to do. These people can provide you with great insight and information about the nature of the work and what they had to do to achieve what they did. While your path may be somewhat different, this type of information can prove invaluable, especially if there is some political work that is needed. Political turf is not always plain to see; and it's good to get the "lay of the land."

Create accountability. One thing about our own personal goals is that there is no one but ourselves to push us and hold us accountable for taking the steps to achieve our goals. There are various things you can do to help you stay true to your commitment, starting with putting dates on your actions or steps. You can also involve someone in your plan such as your boss, mentor or coach. If you ask someone to keep you accountable and ask you about your progress, it will help create a positive "tension" to keep you on task.

Prepare to update your plan. I once heard a saying; "A plan cannot withstand a collision with reality." That means things happen that will cause your plan to stray off of its path. That is natural, but it doesn't mean you shouldn't have a plan. It simply means you need to continually be updating your plan as various circumstances present setbacks or opportunities. I think it is good for you to refresh your plan at least every six months or whenever some significant changes effect either your direction or actions.

The management of your career is your responsibility; and you have to know that it may or may not go anywhere without your guidance. The effort you put into the thinking and ongoing planning will pay you back with the benefit of a career you love. Plus you will feel the direction is largely in your control. Who wouldn't love that?

6 WAYS TO PREPARE YOURSELF FOR THE MANAGEMENT TRACK

MANY PEOPLE ASPIRE to be promoted to a managerial position as the key part of their career goals. It can be very rewarding. Many people are left pondering: How do they get on that management track to begin with? And what do I have to do to prepare? Both good questions. Let's examine what needs to take place to become a manager.

1. **Outline your goals to your management.** Get your boss in your corner to help mentor you and to give you opportunities to prove you are management material.

2. **Look for opportunities to take on more.** A key element to a management position is initiative. You won't be told what to do, you have to assume responsibility and direction. Most groups have far more work than manpower to perform it all. Look for items that will create real impact to the business. Those will get you visibility, which is important to your goals.

3. **Find a role model.** Observe the people who manage and find someone who you believe is both a great manager and is successful. Ask for them to mentor you and observe how they perform their management job, which makes them successful. You want to emulate some of that behavior.

4. **Take classes and read.** There are tons of management classes and books on management. Look for ones that are oriented toward the basics and beginning management, as they will outline what you need to do in these early days. Higher-level materials, while interesting, will assume you know these things and won't go into much detail.

5. **Ask to fill in.** The boss will go on vacation or business travel. They have work to be done while they're away and you can volunteer to cover for them or minimally to pick up some tasks of theirs. This will give you a taste of the work being performed and again demonstrate your ability to take on higher-level responsibilities.

6. **Seek leadership roles.** A great way to get started in management is to take on the role of project management or leader to a work effort. Many of the needed management skills are used in these situations. You are facilitating a group of people to get something accomplished. To do that you will exercise such things as: planning, directing, communicating, gaining agreement, following up and the list goes on. Projects are a key way for business to get done and someone has to lead the effort – that can be you.

If you prepare yourself well, your first management position can be the thing that will catapult you into higher levels and greater impact to your business. You need to make sure that at this stage you have thought through just how different this job is from what you have done before so you can shift gears to be equally awesome as a manager.

ARTICLE #6:

ASKING FOR A PROMOTION IS NOT DICTATED BY TIME ON THE JOB

ASKING FOR A PROMOTION rates right up there with asking for a root canal. Yet, a promotion signifies that our career is growing and moving. It makes us feel good about ourselves and is a form of recognition that our work is worth rewarding.

Still, it can be ponderous when thinking about the details of how and when to ask. It's not something we do every day and we don't always think we know what to do.

There are two things to consider: **1) timing of your performance**, and **2) how to ask**. Let's look at each factor.

1. There is no time interval when it comes to talking about a promotion. However, there are conditions that will dictate the timing:

   • You need to have a clear understanding with the boss on BOTH the deliverables for your current position and the results you need to demonstrate to be at the next level.

   • Assuming you are clear on the above items, you need to be actively seeking feedback from your boss and others that you are meeting or exceeding the expectations of your current job description. This is not to say you must be picture perfect every day. It means you perform your job consistently enough that you are viewed as "rock solid" in doing that work.

- You do have to demonstrate that you can do your job and also perform work at the next level. In other words, you have to prove yourself.

- You should be documenting the job expectations as well as all those various results you obtain. This is important to your next step in asking for a promotion. This information will also reinforce to you when you believe you have consistently performed. Your analysis of this information will help define the time to ask.

2. If you have done all the work mentioned, you don't just run into the boss' office and insist on a promotion. There are conditions you want to look for and preparations that will help ensure your success:

- Be aware of business and personal factors that will impact the decision-making process going on with the boss. If the boss is getting ready or just returned from a vacation or business travel, you don't want to get lost in the frenzy. They have their own workload to think about and they are focusing on the purpose of their travel. Give them space both before and after these events before you approach them. There may be other big deals the boss is working that may not allow them to focus on your request. Pay attention to what is going on with the boss.

- Be aware of your company's business situation. If business has been bad and there is work restructuring or shifting work priorities that has just happened, your request will get lost. Let these things roll out and wait until the dust settles.

- Lay out your case in black and white. You have been documenting your work and expectations, which will help you lay out your case. You don't want to over whelm the boss with too much information, so keep it to the most impactful items making sure you cover all the key expectations your boss has made. You may want to attach copies of emails, especially from the boss that reinforces what you are saying. Be prepared to give a proposed salary increase and don't make it a specific number, but rather a range. Make sure you do your homework so your expectations are appropriate to your company's recent history. This shouldn't be part of your proposal, but may be something you will be asked for. Be prepared to discuss.

- Ask the boss for calendar time. When you do, be prepared to immediately discuss this topic. That makes it important for you to do the previous step before setting up an appointment. When you ask for an appointment, they may schedule out for a month or later today.

- When you meet with them, make a copy of your promotion request for both of you. You want to leave the information with them to read and review after your meeting.

- Do not be defensive, demanding or confrontational in your meeting. Keep your demeanor professional and neutral. You may feel entitled to a promotion, but you definitely don't want to act like it.

- Keep the process accountable. When you've completed your presentation, ask what the next steps and timing are. It's also okay to ask for some general reaction to your request. You will want to know if they disagree and, if so, that turns into a different discussion. Keep in mind that they may not be able to agree right on the spot.

They may need to speak to the big dog or analyze their budget before coming to a decision. Based on what you learn in this step, be prepared to follow up at the time given—not earlier or later.

You can make asking for a promotion more like a professional encounter with your boss with the right kind of advanced planning.

ARTICLE #7:

8 THINGS TO CONSIDER IF YOU WERE PASSED OVER FOR A PROMOTION

AFTER ALL THE hard work, goal setting and focus, you didn't get the promotion you thought would be coming your way. Now you're sitting there wondering what your next move is and whether or not any move would make a difference. This has rocked your world and has left you with more questions than answers.

There are some things for you to do immediately and other things best left to later in the week or next week.

Things to do now:

1. **Stay cool.** The worst thing you could do is stomp into the boss's office and throw what feels like a well-deserved fit. Even if their decision was biased and unfair, a rampage from you won't make your case. It could even be career limiting. If you need to vent, pick someone outside your company who will just let you be however you need to be.

2. **Don't make any big decision.** When we've been hit with a big negative event our brain isn't functioning too well. Simply dig back into your work and let that be your focus for the next week. If you move into action too quickly, it might not be well thought out, which could result in regret. Pick a day for reentering into

the decision and action space. You need time to pull
yourself together.

3. **Don't vent to your peers.** While venting does have its
   merits, right now you shouldn't vent to anyone at
   work. It seems that those conversations have a nasty
   way of making their way to the boss, regardless of
   how close a work peer they might be.

Things to do later—like a week from now:

4. **Clarify the message.** Chances are good that your brain
   shut off the listening function when you heard the
   message you didn't get the promotion. The boss did
   probably give you some important information for
   you to use. Circle back around to any notes or even
   the boss for a quick, clarifying conversation. No
   debate - just gather information.

5. **Move into problem solving.** You have a problem. You
   had expectations of a promotion and you didn't get
   it. This means one of the following:

   a. Expectations of you/the promotion changed
      and you didn't know it.

   b. You weren't communicating well with the
      boss on what it takes and how well you were
      doing.

   c. The decision was arbitrary.

6. **You can't solve a problem you don't fully understand.**
   You also may not be objective enough to completely
   assess the problem. If you have a work mentor, now

is the time to get with them. You need to make sure that whatever action you take will truly address the underlying problem. If you executed the previous step, you should have some good information that will shed light on the problem you need to fix.

7. **Get the right attitude.** You aren't "owed" a promotion. You need to take the approach that you will make adjustments that will put you on the right track. Don't over compensate, simply resolve that this is a problem to solve. It also doesn't mean that you aren't worthy of a promotion, so don't act like a whipped dog.

8. **What if this is impossible?** If this isn't the first time for being passed over, then it is time for you to rethink your future at this company. If you are being realistic about your performance and capability and if your promotion is long overdue, it's time to leave. Sometimes we don't mesh with what the company values. You might be a great performer, but you aren't material for upper levels with this company. That's okay to know. You will do better somewhere else. It doesn't mean you're not worthy. You are; just not here. Time to go.

Don't let this derail you or your career goals. Learn from this situation and take the right actions that will get you where you know you can go.

Conclusion

FOLLOWING THE STEPS I've outlined in this book will lead you to long-lasting career success and satisfaction. It's never too late to start planning your next step. As we age, our interests change, we strengthen our abilities and we tend to know ourselves better.

What you trained for at age twenty may be completely

obsolete now. Or you may have lost your passion for it. What I do know is that there is always a place for someone who continues to grow and learn, someone who develops their skills. Every person has a value they bring to the marketplace.

If you're looking for help, guidance or advice, consider my coaching program. You'll discover the many fascinating ways to deliver your value to the workforce and to your personal life as well.

To work with Dorothy Tannahill-Moran, contact her at Dorothy@introvertwhisperer.com

WOULD YOU PLEASE REVIEW?

WOULD YOU BE SO KIND as to leave a book review? Authors books have a much better chance at being successful when the readers share that they've enjoyed reading the book and/or found it helpful . . . which I hope you did. If you could take a few minutes to leave a review, I'd appreciate it ever so much.

VIDEO SERIES

Get Free Instant Access to Video series,

"The 5 Most Common Ways Introverts Commit Career Self-Sabotage and How to Avoid Them"

These videos are designed to accelerate your results
with **CAREER MAPPING**,
and are my way of saying "thank you" for purchasing this book.

www.introvertwhisperer.com/career goals

OTHER BOOKS FROM
DOROTHY TANNAHILL-MORAN

Easier Networking
for Introverts and the Socially Reluctant:
A 4-Step Guide That's Natural, Stress-Free and Gets Results

———

Elevator Speeches
That Get Results

———

Personal Branding:
A Simple Guide to Reinvent & Manage Your Brand
for Career Success

———

Accelerate your Career
(Even with a Bad Boss):
A New Approach to Managing Up

ABOUT THE AUTHOR

Dorothy Tannahill-Moran is *The Introvert Whisperer,* a leadership and career coach, author and speaker. Born an introvert, then shaped into a leader, she is a delightful fusion of unique, useful insight and rock-solid management expertise. As a Career Coach, she guides the reluctant toward better relationships with their boss and management, teaching introverts how to effectively collaborate with difficult people, navigate workplace culture and internal politics, and successfully network in a room filled with strangers. This is why Dorothy Tannhill-Moran is a sought-out and trusted advisor to corporate professionals and executives worldwide.

A graduate of Emporia State University with a Bachelor of Science in Education, Dorothy was recruited by the Kansas City School District to coordinate their Distributive Education program. Four years later, she was hired by Intel where she quickly rose through their ranks to senior-level management. With over twenty-one years supervising Intel's diverse staff mix, she coached, guided and trained others at all levels to achieve impressive careers, executive status, higher salaries, while gaining broad professional recognition. Twice, Intel bestowed upon her their highest achievement award, spotlighting her outstanding accomplishments and the positive, long-lasting impact she made on their culture.

For more powerful career strategies, go to:

www.introvertwhisperer.com

ACKNOWLEDGEMENTS

WHEN I STARTED WRITING this book, I didn't realize I was writing a book until long after I finished the manuscript. For some reason, I thought I was writing an "e-product" for people to download, which is still true, only now I realize it's also a book. Interesting how our minds work.

My journey to this place starts with the tireless support of my husband, Terry Moran, who has believed in me for some thirty-plus years and given me strength. Until he came into my life, I didn't realize how much one person's belief in another could help you jump hurtles you didn't know you could.

My deceased mother, Mildred Tannahill, who's wisdom shaped me and rings true every day. She should have been an author, because she wrote for as long as I could remember and she truly wanted to give a voice to her ideas. I have a box full of her work and perhaps one day when I figure all of this out, she will finally get published.

To my BFF, Ruth Colter, who is herself an author of *Zelfar, The Discovery* and a source of inspiration. Ruth is the perpetual up-beat person in my life and is always sure that the right things come your way.

Lastly, I have to thank and honor my clients who I have seen work hard on their career goals and prevail. They are the daily testimony that to love your job is to love your life. My clients make all of this exciting and fun each and every day I am honored to spend time with them.

73744048R00065

Made in the USA
Columbia, SC
06 September 2019